Ange

Healing

40 Days

Of

Enlightenment

SM

Written By
Rev. Debbie Michaels

. . . and I shall send you angels
to guard you, to guide you,
and to bless you
Indeed

Angelic-Reiki Energy Healing

40 Days
Of
Enlightenment

Contact the author at…
www.WhereAngelsGather.org
angelsgather88@hotmail.com

Contents

The following pages contain four powerful ten
day meditations; along with the meditations is
a ten day guide of journal; for each
Meditation.
Use these meditations wisely, they come from
the Angelic-Reiki Realm of Angels and hold
the power to change your life.

By the Grace of God,
Go I

SM

The top symbol represents

GOD

Our Divine Creator

The other symbol represents

GRACE

May the Grace of God find favor in you.

This Sacred Journal

Belongs to

_____

天
恩

Angelic-Reiki Energy Healing

Healing

40 Days

Of

Enlightenment

Meditation of Joy

Angelic-Reiki Healing Angels'
Meditation of Joy

Please do this Meditation for the next Ten days.

This Meditation is used for your personal healing.

To prepare, Invoke: the *Angelic-Reiki Healing Angels* **and** *Archangel Raphael.* Ask them to help open you to their *Healing Energy* and to support you through the healing process.

Sit comfortably where you will not be disturbed. Begin by grounding and centering yourself. Close your eyes and imagine roots growing from your feet into the Earth.

Follow this simple breathing exercise to relax your physical body: breathe in through your nose, hold it for several seconds, and release it very slowly through your mouth.

Continue breathing this way throughout the meditation.

Ask *The Divine Creator* to send down a beam of protective white light. Envision a beam of light coming down from the Heavens. Watch it surround you, placing you in a protective sphere.

This Sphere of White Light is protecting you.

In all time, all realms, and all space.

I sit in a relaxed position; my body slowly fills with Angelic-Reiki Healing Energy. I quiet myself and I find inner-peace, the journey of my life is unique and filled with wonder. Beauty surrounds me; life's tranquility and harmony are mine. I go peacefully amid the noise of the world, and I remember the beauty of creation, each flower blooming, and each drop of rain that falls. I am blessed with the knowledge of continual growth, continual wisdom, and continual enlightenment.

I surrender myself to be at peace with the human realm, with each and every person; opening my inner self to humanity. I speak of love, I speak of truth, and I speak clearly.

I also listen to each and every person for in the simplest of stories may hold the secrets of life. I accept counsel surrendering to the wisdom of the ages; for each of us carries our own story of life; our own truth.

I remain open to others, keeping myself open to wisdom; I stay humble and grateful, as my life unfolds.

I am cautious with each step I take, that I may not stumble. Yet I go forth with my eyes open, knowing that virtue and bravery may be found in each and every one.

I stay open to love and strive to keep my compassion. I open my arms to receive affections.

For love is found in each smile, each act of kindness, and each gentle touch. I am not alone.

Though I may not understand all, I yield to the unfolding of my life and I am at peace.

I am blessed indeed, for I am a child of God.

I am of Happiness.

I am of Joy.

And

I am Grateful.

Rev. Debbie Michaels
September 17, 2011

Day 1

I focused on the realization of the Angelic-Reiki Realm of Healing Angels and the healing of my soul:

_____

_____

_____

_____

_____

_____

_____

_____

_____

_____

_____

_____

_____

_____

_____

_____

_____

_____

_____

_____

天
恩

Images I received during my Healing Focus:

_____

_____

_____

_____

_____

_____

_____

_____

_____

_____

_____

_____

_____

_____

_____

_____

_____

_____

_____

_____

_____

_____

_____

_____

_____

_____

I quieted myself and received these messages:

_____
_____
_____
_____
_____
_____
_____
_____
_____
_____
_____
_____
_____
_____
_____
_____
_____
_____
_____
_____
_____
_____
_____
_____
_____
_____
_____

Day 2

I focused on the realization of the Angelic-Reiki Realm of Healing Angels and the healing of my soul:

_____

_____

_____

_____

_____

_____

_____

_____

_____

_____

_____

_____

_____

_____

_____

_____

_____

_____

_____

_____

_____

_____

_____

_____

_____

天
恩

Images I received during my Healing Focus:

I quieted myself and received these messages:

_____

_____

_____

_____

_____

_____

_____

_____

_____

_____

_____

_____

_____

_____

_____

_____

_____

_____

_____

_____

_____

_____

_____

_____

_____

Day 3

I focused on the realization of the Angelic-Reiki Realm of Healing Angels and the healing of my soul:

天
恩

Images I received during my Healing Focus:

_____

_____

_____

_____

_____

_____

_____

_____

_____

_____

_____

_____

_____

_____

_____

_____

_____

_____

_____

_____

_____

_____

_____

_____

_____

_____

_____

_____

I quieted myself and received these messages:

_____

_____

_____

_____

_____

_____

_____

_____

_____

_____

_____

_____

_____

_____

_____

_____

_____

_____

_____

_____

_____

_____

_____

_____

Day 4

I focused on the realization of the Angelic-Reiki Realm of Healing Angels and the healing of my soul:

天
恩

Images I received during my Healing Focus:

_____

_____

_____

_____

_____

_____

_____

_____

_____

_____

_____

_____

_____

_____

_____

_____

_____

_____

_____

_____

_____

_____

_____

_____

_____

_____

I quieted myself and received these messages:

_____

_____

_____

_____

_____

_____

_____

_____

_____

_____

_____

_____

_____

_____

_____

_____

_____

_____

_____

_____

_____

_____

_____

_____

_____

_____

_____

Day 5

I focused on the realization of the Angelic-Reiki Realm of Healing Angels and the healing of my soul:

天
恩

Images I received during my Healing Focus:

_____

_____

_____

_____

_____

_____

_____

_____

_____

_____

_____

_____

_____

_____

_____

_____

_____

_____

_____

_____

_____

_____

_____

_____

_____

_____

_____

_____

I quieted myself and received these messages:

_____

_____

_____

_____

_____

_____

_____

_____

_____

_____

_____

_____

_____

_____

_____

_____

_____

_____

_____

_____

_____

_____

_____

_____

_____

_____

_____

Day 6

I focused on the realization of the Angelic-Reiki Realm of Healing Angels and the healing of my soul:

天
恩

Images I received during my Healing Focus:

_____

_____

_____

_____

_____

_____

_____

_____

_____

_____

_____

_____

_____

_____

_____

_____

_____

_____

_____

_____

_____

_____

_____

_____

_____

_____

I quieted myself and received these messages:

_____

_____

_____

_____

_____

_____

_____

_____

_____

_____

_____

_____

_____

_____

_____

_____

_____

_____

_____

_____

_____

_____

_____

Day 7

I focused on the realization of the Angelic-Reiki Realm of Healing Angels and the healing of my soul:

天
恩

Images I received during my Healing Focus:

_____

_____

_____

_____

_____

_____

_____

_____

_____

_____

_____

_____

_____

_____

_____

_____

_____

_____

_____

_____

_____

_____

_____

_____

_____

I quieted myself and received these messages:

_____

_____

_____

_____

_____

_____

_____

_____

_____

_____

_____

_____

_____

_____

_____

_____

_____

_____

_____

_____

_____

_____

_____

Day 8

I focused on the realization of the Angelic-Reiki Realm of Healing Angels and the healing of my soul:

天
恩

Images I received during my Healing Focus:

_____

_____

_____

_____

_____

_____

_____

_____

_____

_____

_____

_____

_____

_____

_____

_____

_____

_____

_____

_____

_____

_____

_____

_____

_____

_____

I quieted myself and received these messages:

_____
_____
_____
_____
_____
_____
_____
_____
_____
_____
_____
_____
_____
_____
_____
_____
_____
_____
_____
_____
_____
_____
_____
_____
_____
_____

Day 9

I focused on the realization of the Angelic-Reiki Realm of Healing Angels and the healing of my soul:_____

_____

_____

_____

_____

_____

_____

_____

_____

_____

_____

_____

_____

_____

_____

_____

_____

_____

_____

_____

_____

_____

_____

天
恩

Images I received during my Healing Focus:

_____

_____

_____

_____

_____

_____

_____

_____

_____

_____

_____

_____

_____

_____

_____

_____

_____

_____

_____

_____

_____

_____

_____

_____

_____

_____

_____

I quieted myself and received these messages:

_____

_____

_____

_____

_____

_____

_____

_____

_____

_____

_____

_____

_____

_____

_____

_____

_____

_____

_____

_____

_____

_____

_____

_____

_____

_____

Day 10

I focused on the realization of the Angelic-Reiki Realm of Healing Angels and the healing of my soul:

天恩

Images I received during my Healing Focus:

_____

_____

_____

_____

_____

_____

_____

_____

_____

_____

_____

_____

_____

_____

_____

_____

_____

_____

_____

_____

_____

_____

_____

_____

_____

_____

_____

_____

I quieted myself and received these messages:

_____

_____

_____

_____

_____

_____

_____

_____

_____

_____

_____

_____

_____

_____

_____

_____

_____

_____

_____

_____

_____

_____

_____

_____

Meditation for Astral Travel

Angelic-Reiki Healing Angels' Meditation for Astral Travel

Please do this Meditation for the next Ten days.

This Meditation is used for your personal healing.

To prepare, Invoke: the *Angelic-Reiki Healing Angels* **and** *Archangel Raphael.* Ask them to help open you to their *Healing Energy* and to support you through the healing process.

Sit comfortably where you will not be disturbed. Begin by grounding and centering yourself. Close your eyes and imagine roots growing from your feet into the Earth.

Follow this simple breathing exercise to relax your physical body: breathe in through your nose, hold it for several seconds, and release it very slowly through your mouth.

Continue breathing this way throughout the meditation.

Ask *The Divine Creator* to send down a beam of protective white light. Envision a beam of light coming down from the Heavens. Watch it surround you, placing you in a protective sphere.

This Sphere of White Light is protecting you.

In all time, all realms, and all space.

As I sit comfortably I become aware of myself, my soul, I am quiet and at peace.

My physical body fills with Angelic-Reiki Light a halo of white light forms around me and through me.

I form in my mind's eye, my true self a body of light; no longer bound by the physical.

As I become confident in my light body, I realize I may separate from the physical, without disconnecting.

I feel a freedom from physical limitations, I am free, I slowly move upward gently away from my physical body. I am above myself.

I look at my hand, these beautiful hands of light. I am at peace; I feel a freedom I have never felt before.

All limitations are gone.

I feel a hand take mine, I look up, it is a golden being of light. It is my guide from the Angelic-Reiki realm.

I feel angelic essence fill my light body and begin to radiate a golden glow.

I move freely as a bird in flight. I move confidently and calmly.

My guide asks where I would like to go, and what would I like to see. I can travel anywhere with my guide.

I focus on a location and in a second I am there.

I look around and am infused with its wisdom; soaring through time and space I radiate love and happiness.

While I am still with my guide, I visit people who welcome me.

I bestow upon them the love and happiness I am radiating.

I part form them and return to my physical body.

I float gently into my physical body, as I return to it I thank my guide for sharing the golden light of love and peace.

My guide tells me I may journey like this at any time, but only within the golden light.

I am also asked to write down all my experiences for I have just begun my journey.

I am filled with thoughts as I breathe deeply.

I begin to journal my experiences.

Rev. Debbie Michaels
September 17, 2011

Day 11

I focused on the realization of the Angelic-Reiki Realm of Healing Angels and the wisdom I received during my Astral-Travel:

_____

_____

_____

_____

_____

_____

_____

_____

_____

_____

_____

_____

_____

_____

_____

_____

_____

_____

_____

_____

_____

_____

_____

_____

天
恩

Images I received during my Astral-Travel:

_____

_____

_____

_____

_____

_____

_____

_____

_____

_____

_____

_____

_____

_____

_____

_____

_____

_____

_____

_____

_____

_____

_____

_____

_____

_____

_____

_____

_____

_____

I quieted myself and received these messages:

_____

_____

_____

_____

_____

_____

_____

_____

_____

_____

_____

_____

_____

_____

_____

_____

_____

_____

_____

_____

_____

_____

_____

_____

_____

_____

Day 12

I focused on the realization of the Angelic-Reiki Realm of Healing Angels and the wisdom I received during my Astral-Travel:

_____
_____
_____
_____
_____
_____
_____
_____
_____
_____
_____
_____
_____
_____
_____
_____
_____
_____
_____
_____
_____
_____
_____
_____

天
恩

Images I received during my Astral-Travel:

I quieted myself and received these messages:

_____

_____

_____

_____

_____

_____

_____

_____

_____

_____

_____

_____

_____

_____

_____

_____

_____

_____

_____

_____

_____

_____

_____

_____

Day 13

I focused on the realization of the Angelic-Reiki Realm of Healing Angels and the wisdom I received during my Astral-Travel:

天
恩

Images I received during my Astral-Travel:

_____

_____

_____

_____

_____

_____

_____

_____

_____

_____

_____

_____

_____

_____

_____

_____

_____

_____

_____

_____

_____

_____

_____

_____

_____

_____

_____

I quieted myself and received these messages:

_____
_____
_____
_____
_____
_____
_____
_____
_____
_____
_____
_____
_____
_____
_____
_____
_____
_____
_____
_____
_____
_____
_____
_____
_____
_____
_____

Day 14

I focused on the realization of the Angelic-Reiki Realm of Healing Angels and the wisdom I received during my Astral-Travel:

天
恩

Images I received during my Astral-Travel:

_____

_____

_____

_____

_____

_____

_____

_____

_____

_____

_____

_____

_____

_____

_____

_____

_____

_____

_____

_____

_____

_____

_____

_____

_____

_____

I quieted myself and received these messages:

Day 15

I focused on the realization of the Angelic-Reiki Realm of Healing Angels and the wisdom I received during my Astral-Travel:

天
恩

Images I received during my Astral-Travel:

_____

_____

_____

_____

_____

_____

_____

_____

_____

_____

_____

_____

_____

_____

_____

_____

_____

_____

_____

_____

_____

_____

_____

_____

_____

_____

_____

_____

_____

I quieted myself and received these messages:

Day 16

I focused on the realization of the Angelic-Reiki Realm of Healing Angels and the wisdom I received during my Astral-Travel:

天
恩

Images I received during my Astral-Travel:

_____

_____

_____

_____

_____

_____

_____

_____

_____

_____

_____

_____

_____

_____

_____

_____

_____

_____

_____

_____

_____

_____

_____

_____

_____

_____

_____

_____

_____

I quieted myself and received these messages:

_____

_____

_____

_____

_____

_____

_____

_____

_____

_____

_____

_____

_____

_____

_____

_____

_____

_____

_____

_____

_____

_____

_____

_____

_____

_____

_____

Day 17

I focused on the realization of the Angelic-Reiki Realm of Healing Angels and the wisdom I received during my Astral-Travel:

天
恩

Images I received during my Astral-Travel:

_____

_____

_____

_____

_____

_____

_____

_____

_____

_____

_____

_____

_____

_____

_____

_____

_____

_____

_____

_____

_____

_____

_____

_____

_____

_____

_____

I quieted myself and received these messages:

_____

_____

_____

_____

_____

_____

_____

_____

_____

_____

_____

_____

_____

_____

_____

_____

_____

_____

_____

_____

_____

_____

_____

_____

_____

_____

_____

Day 18

I focused on the realization of the Angelic-Reiki Realm of Healing Angels and the wisdom I received during my Astral-Travel:

天
恩

Images I received during my Astral-Travel:

I quieted myself and received these messages:

Day 19

I focused on the realization of the Angelic-Reiki Realm of Healing Angels and the wisdom I received during my Astral-Travel:

天
恩

Images I received during my Astral-Travel:

I quieted myself and received these messages:

_____

_____

_____

_____

_____

_____

_____

_____

_____

_____

_____

_____

_____

_____

_____

_____

_____

_____

_____

_____

_____

_____

_____

_____

_____

_____

_____

Day 20

I focused on the realization of the Angelic-Reiki Realm of Healing Angels and the wisdom I received during my Astral-Travel:

天
恩

Images I received during my Astral-Travel:

_____

_____

_____

_____

_____

_____

_____

_____

_____

_____

_____

_____

_____

_____

_____

_____

_____

_____

_____

_____

_____

_____

_____

_____

_____

_____

_____

I quieted myself and received these messages:

_____

_____

_____

_____

_____

_____

_____

_____

_____

_____

_____

_____

_____

_____

_____

_____

_____

_____

_____

_____

_____

_____

_____

_____

_____

_____

_____

Meditation for Relaxation

Angelic-Reiki Healing Angels' Meditation for Relaxation

Please do this Meditation for the next Ten days.

This Meditation is used for your personal healing.

To prepare, Invoke: the *Angelic-Reiki Healing Angels* and *Archangel Raphael.* Ask them to help open you to their *Healing Energy* and to support you through the healing process.

Sit comfortably where you will not be disturbed. Begin by grounding and centering yourself. Close your eyes and imagine roots growing from your feet into the Earth.

Follow this simple breathing exercise to relax your physical body: breathe in through your nose, hold it for several seconds, and release it very slowly through your mouth.

Continue breathing this way throughout the meditation.

Ask *The Divine Creator* to send down a beam of protective white light. Envision a beam of light coming down from the Heavens. Watch it surround you, placing you in a protective sphere.

This Sphere of White Light is protecting you.

In all time, all realms, and all space.

Once more I come to sit quietly and to quiet myself. I relax my mind, I release all stress. I remove the friction, the tug of war with decisions in my life, I am at peace.

I find myself sitting beside a flowing stream, the water move slowly and gently. My worries flow along within the water.

The thoughts of my life come into focus, my problems, I can see them clearly, I am no longer confused. I am no longer afraid. For along with those problems I see the solutions floating nearby. Simple solutions that I had not thought of before; I smile.

I realize how unnecessary it was for me to worry; now I will relax.

Sitting on the bank of the stream I watch them float away as each solution connects to the problem.

I am an observer of my life, knowing that with the asking for Divine Intervention, the solutions connect faster to the problems. Dissolving each problem one at a time; the stream becomes clear water.

I enjoy the beauty of the clear stream, knowing that the stream is my life. I feel the warmth of the sun upon my face; it is the warmth of blessings being bestowed upon me.

And now I breathe in accepting the blessings and knowledge of the solutions.

I am grateful and

Once more I begin to journal.

Rev. Debbie Michaels
September 17, 2011

Day 21

I focused on the realization of the Angelic-Reiki Realm of Healing Angels and the peace are harmony of my soul:

天恩

Solutions, I received during my meditation.

_____
_____
_____
_____
_____
_____
_____
_____
_____
_____
_____
_____
_____
_____
_____
_____
_____
_____
_____
_____
_____
_____
_____
_____
_____
_____
_____
_____
_____

I quieted myself and received these messages:

Day 22

I focused on the realization of the Angelic-Reiki Realm of Healing Angels and the peace are harmony of my soul:

天
恩

Solutions, I received during my meditation.

_____

_____

_____

_____

_____

_____

_____

_____

_____

_____

_____

_____

_____

_____

_____

_____

_____

_____

_____

_____

_____

_____

_____

_____

_____

_____

_____

_____

_____

I quieted myself and received these messages:

_____

_____

_____

_____

_____

_____

_____

_____

_____

_____

_____

_____

_____

_____

_____

_____

_____

_____

_____

_____

_____

_____

_____

_____

_____

_____

_____

_____

Day 23

I focused on the realization of the Angelic-Reiki Realm of Healing Angels and the peace are harmony of my soul:

天
恩

Solutions, I received during my meditation.

_____
_____
_____
_____
_____
_____
_____
_____
_____
_____
_____
_____
_____
_____
_____
_____
_____
_____
_____
_____
_____
_____
_____
_____
_____
_____
_____
_____

I quieted myself and received these messages:

_____

_____

_____

_____

_____

_____

_____

_____

_____

_____

_____

_____

_____

_____

_____

_____

_____

_____

_____

_____

_____

_____

_____

_____

_____

Day 24

I focused on the realization of the Angelic-Reiki Realm of Healing Angels and the peace are harmony of my soul:

天
恩

Solutions, I received during my meditation.

_____

_____

_____

_____

_____

_____

_____

_____

_____

_____

_____

_____

_____

_____

_____

_____

_____

_____

_____

_____

_____

_____

_____

_____

_____

_____

_____

I quieted myself and received these messages:

_____

_____

_____

_____

_____

_____

_____

_____

_____

_____

_____

_____

_____

_____

_____

_____

_____

_____

_____

_____

_____

_____

_____

_____

_____

_____

_____

Day 25

I focused on the realization of the Angelic-Reiki Realm of Healing Angels and the peace are harmony of my soul:

天
恩

Solutions, I received during my meditation.

_____

_____

_____

_____

_____

_____

_____

_____

_____

_____

_____

_____

_____

_____

_____

_____

_____

_____

_____

_____

_____

_____

_____

_____

_____

_____

_____

I quieted myself and received these messages:

_____

_____

_____

_____

_____

_____

_____

_____

_____

_____

_____

_____

_____

_____

_____

_____

_____

_____

_____

_____

_____

_____

_____

_____

_____

_____

_____

_____

Day 26

I focused on the realization of the Angelic-Reiki Realm of Healing Angels and the peace are harmony of my soul:

天
恩

Solutions, I received during my meditation.

I quieted myself and received these messages:

_____

_____

_____

_____

_____

_____

_____

_____

_____

_____

_____

_____

_____

_____

_____

_____

_____

_____

_____

_____

_____

_____

_____

_____

_____

_____

Day 27

I focused on the realization of the Angelic-Reiki Realm of Healing Angels and the peace are harmony of my soul:

天
恩

Solutions, I received during my meditation.

I quieted myself and received these messages:

_____

_____

_____

_____

_____

_____

_____

_____

_____

_____

_____

_____

_____

_____

_____

_____

_____

_____

_____

_____

_____

_____

_____

_____

_____

_____

_____

Day 28

I focused on the realization of the Angelic-Reiki Realm of Healing Angels and the peace are harmony of my soul:

天
恩

Solutions, I received during my meditation.

_____

_____

_____

_____

_____

_____

_____

_____

_____

_____

_____

_____

_____

_____

_____

_____

_____

_____

_____

_____

_____

_____

_____

_____

I quieted myself and received these messages:

Day 29

I focused on the realization of the Angelic-Reiki Realm of Healing Angels and the peace are harmony of my soul:

天
恩

Solutions, I received during my meditation.

I quieted myself and received these messages:

Day 30

I focused on the realization of the Angelic-Reiki Realm of Healing Angels and the peace are harmony of my soul:

天
恩

Solutions, I received during my meditation.

_____

_____

_____

_____

_____

_____

_____

_____

_____

_____

_____

_____

_____

_____

_____

_____

_____

_____

_____

_____

_____

_____

_____

_____

I quieted myself and received these messages:

Meditation for Prosperity

Angelic-Reiki Healing Angels' Meditation for Prosperity

Please do this Meditation for the next Ten days.

This Meditation is used for your personal healing.

To prepare, Invoke: the *Angelic-Reiki Healing Angels* and *Archangel Raphael.* Ask them to help open you to their *Healing Energy* and to support you through the healing process.

Sit comfortably where you will not be disturbed. Begin by grounding and centering yourself. Close your eyes and imagine roots growing from your feet into the Earth.

Follow this simple breathing exercise to relax your physical body: breathe in through your nose, hold it for several seconds, and release it very slowly through your mouth.

Continue breathing this way throughout the meditation.

Ask *The Divine Creator* to send down a beam of protective white light. Envision a beam of light coming down from the Heavens. Watch it surround you, placing you in a protective sphere.

This Sphere of White Light is protecting you.

In all time, all realms, and all space.

I sit quietly and relaxed. I am at peace with myself. I love myself just the way I am, I am a beautiful being of light I radiate joy and harmony.

My thoughts begin to flow moving slowly, yet in constant motion. I have thought of positive ventures. I create the energy of joy. My mind is filled with positive energy, as each thought becomes clearer, the negative thoughts dissipate.

I embrace the Angels of the Angelic-Reiki Realm; their healing energies engulf me. Their warmth heals my mind and destroys all negative thoughts. The Angels bring with them comfort. I find myself at peace. I focus on good health, mental clarity, and love. I am restored. I replace any and all negative thoughts with the truth, that with Divine Intervention all things are possible.

I am empowered with this knowledge.

I am confident in this knowledge.

For this is truth; I am a powerful being filled with Angelic-Reiki Energy and all things are possible.

I am carefree; I am beyond the chaos of life. I create positive thought and create my world in a positive way; with joy and love.

As I breathe in this wondrous knowledge it is infused into my being.

All things are possible, I take a breath.

All things are possible, I take another breath.

All things are possible; I take in the breath of this knowledge.

This knowledge illuminates me.

I am a magnate of prosperity.

Prosperity in abundance.

Now and forever.

Rev. Debbie Michaels
September 17, 2011

Day 31

I focused on the realization of the Angelic-Reiki Realm of Healing Angels the Abundance of Life::

天
恩

Images I received during my meditation focus:

I quieted myself and received these messages:

_____

_____

_____

_____

_____

_____

_____

_____

_____

_____

_____

_____

_____

_____

_____

_____

_____

_____

_____

_____

_____

_____

_____

_____

_____

_____

_____

_____

Day 32

I focused on the realization of the Angelic-Reiki Realm of Healing Angels the Abundance of Life::

天恩

Images I received during my meditation focus:

I quieted myself and received these messages:

Day 33

I focused on the realization of the Angelic-Reiki Realm of Healing Angels the Abundance of Life::

天
恩

Images I received during my meditation focus:

_____

_____

_____

_____

_____

_____

_____

_____

_____

_____

_____

_____

_____

_____

_____

_____

_____

_____

_____

_____

_____

_____

_____

_____

_____

_____

_____

I quieted myself and received these messages:

_____

_____

_____

_____

_____

_____

_____

_____

_____

_____

_____

_____

_____

_____

_____

_____

_____

_____

_____

_____

_____

_____

_____

_____

_____

_____

Day 34

I focused on the realization of the Angelic-Reiki Realm of Healing Angels the Abundance of Life::

天
恩

Images I received during my meditation focus:

_____

_____

_____

_____

_____

_____

_____

_____

_____

_____

_____

_____

_____

_____

_____

_____

_____

_____

_____

_____

_____

_____

_____

_____

_____

_____

I quieted myself and received these messages:

_____

_____

_____

_____

_____

_____

_____

_____

_____

_____

_____

_____

_____

_____

_____

_____

_____

_____

_____

_____

_____

_____

_____

_____

Day 35

I focused on the realization of the Angelic-Reiki Realm of Healing Angels the Abundance of Life::

天
恩

Images I received during my meditation focus:

_____

_____

_____

_____

_____

_____

_____

_____

_____

_____

_____

_____

_____

_____

_____

_____

_____

_____

_____

_____

_____

_____

_____

_____

_____

I quieted myself and received these messages:

_____

_____

_____

_____

_____

_____

_____

_____

_____

_____

_____

_____

_____

_____

_____

_____

_____

_____

_____

_____

_____

_____

_____

_____

_____

_____

Day 36

I focused on the realization of the Angelic-Reiki Realm of Healing Angels the Abundance of Life::

天
恩

Images I received during my meditation focus:

_____

_____

_____

_____

_____

_____

_____

_____

_____

_____

_____

_____

_____

_____

_____

_____

_____

_____

_____

_____

_____

_____

_____

_____

_____

_____

I quieted myself and received these messages:

_____

_____

_____

_____

_____

_____

_____

_____

_____

_____

_____

_____

_____

_____

_____

_____

_____

_____

_____

_____

_____

_____

_____

_____

_____

<u>Day 37</u>

I focused on the realization of the Angelic-Reiki Realm of Healing Angels the Abundance of Life::_____

天
恩

Images I received during my meditation focus:

_____

_____

_____

_____

_____

_____

_____

_____

_____

_____

_____

_____

_____

_____

_____

_____

_____

_____

_____

_____

_____

_____

_____

_____

_____

_____

_____

_____

I quieted myself and received these messages:

Day 38

I focused on the realization of the Angelic-Reiki Realm of Healing Angels the Abundance of Life::

天
恩

Images I received during my meditation focus:

_____
_____
_____
_____
_____
_____
_____
_____
_____
_____
_____
_____
_____
_____
_____
_____
_____
_____
_____
_____
_____
_____
_____
_____
_____
_____
_____

I quieted myself and received these messages:

<u>Day 39</u>

I focused on the realization of the Angelic-Reiki Realm of Healing Angels the Abundance of Life::_____

_____

_____

_____

_____

_____

_____

_____

_____

_____

_____

_____

_____

_____

_____

_____

_____

_____

_____

_____

_____

_____

天
恩

Images I received during my meditation focus:

_____

_____

_____

_____

_____

_____

_____

_____

_____

_____

_____

_____

_____

_____

_____

_____

_____

_____

_____

_____

_____

_____

_____

_____

_____

_____

_____

_____

I quieted myself and received these messages:

Day 40

I focused on the realization of the Angelic-Reiki Realm of Healing Angels the Abundance of Life::

天
恩

Images I received during my meditation focus:

I quieted myself and received these messages:

_____

_____

_____

_____

_____

_____

_____

_____

_____

_____

_____

_____

_____

_____

_____

_____

_____

_____

_____

_____

_____

_____

_____

_____

_____

My Wish for You

As Always...

May The Powers That Be

Bless You Indeed

With health, wealth

And prosperity

With

Wisdom to share

And

Courage to lead

May They guard your gate

Always keeping safe

Your fate.

Rev. Debbie Michaels

Manufactured by Amazon.ca
Acheson, AB